Y0-BTU-869

52 nice things to do to make someone happy

Jeri-Lynn Johnson

Visit us at www.shadowmountain.com

Library of Congress Cataloging-in-Publication Data

Johnson, Jeri-Lynn, 1945-
Fifty-two nice things to do to make someone happy / Jeri-Lynn Johnson.
p. cm.
ISBN 1-57345-917-8 (pbk.)
1. Female friendship. 2. Friendship.

I. Title.

BJ1533.F8 J64 2001
158.2'5--dc21 2001000395

Printed in the United States of America 54459-6790

10 9 8 7 6 5 4 3 2 1

To all my friends and family members who have been my inspiration. I made these notes while observing how you treat others. You have made me want to be like you.

PREFACE

Do you have or have you ever had a *real* friend? Someone who cares as much about you as she does about herself? If not, wouldn't it be wonderful to have someone in your life upon whom you could depend? Someone whose loyalty and love could not be questioned?

There's an old saying: "If you want to have a friend, you must first be a friend." The reason this saying is still around is that it is true. My purpose in writing this book is to help you be the best friend you can be.

You may never do anything more important than extend a kindness to another human being, especially if that person sees no light at the end of his tunnel, has given up hope, or has no expectation that relief is available. In these lines, Alexander Pope suggests that such an act may even have eternal significance:

What we have done for ourselves alone dies
with us.
What we have done for others and the world remains
and is immortal.

This book, then, is for you. And for your friend.

1. I've found that the number one nice thing you can do for a friend is listen to her. Really listen to her. It sounds easy, but the next time you and a friend are talking, pay attention to your conversation. Who is doing all the talking? And while listening, are you thinking about what you are going to say next? Resolve to let your friend do the talking and you listen. Ask questions. Be genuinely interested in what she is telling you.

2. Listen for specific needs people have and then figure out a way to meet them. I prefer to do nice things anonymously, but if you are trying to develop a friendship, you probably want the person to know that you are the one who is making the effort to help. Helping others brings people closer. You can't help but feel closer to someone who has done you a favor. The same goes for the person who is doing the favor. It works both ways.

3. Find a way to tell the person how much he means to you. Explain how he has influenced your life and what you admire most about him. If this is too uncomfortable for you, go on to #4 and express your feelings in a card or letter. Life is short—and unpredictable. A common regret among mourners after a friend has passed away is that the mourner neglected to express appreciation to the deceased person before it was too late.

4. Get in touch with old friends. E-mail your old associates. Write a letter or send a card to friends that you haven't heard from. Let them know you still think of them. If you hear good or bad news about a friend, send her a note. Don't know what to say? Get a copy of Joyce Landorf Heatherley's book *Special Words: Notes for When You Don't Know What to Say*. She'll put some appropriate words in your mouth.

5. Ask a friend to do *you* a favor (drive your carpool, take you to a doctor's appointment, etc.). I know, none of us likes to ask people to do anything for us. But if we don't, we are denying them the good feelings that come from helping others. We can't always be on the giving end; we need to allow others to serve us. We need to learn how to graciously receive as well. A simple "thank you" is a gracious response and so much better than protesting about why she shouldn't have done it. Think

of the chance to accept help as a bonding opportunity. Your friend will feel closer to you because you asked her and not someone else.

6. Borrow something (sugar, eggs, etc., but not money). This gives you an opportunity to check on your friend to see how she is doing and allows time for comfortable, nonthreatening conversation. Don't forget to return the item. If you borrowed sugar, eggs, or milk, it would be a nice gesture to return it along with a

home-baked goodie for your friend to enjoy. It's a thoughtful thing to put your goodie in a throw-away tin, so she doesn't have to remember or bother to get a dish or plate back to you.

7. Show up at your friend's house and say, "I'm yours for two hours, what have you got for me to do?" She probably won't dare suggest a thing, so be prepared to be specific. "Let me do your ironing," or "Let me

wash your windows." Or you could bring over some spring bulbs to plant in her garden. This is an especially nice gesture if you know your friend is expecting house guests or is planning a wedding and could use some extra help getting ready for the event. If you are still at a loss for something to do and your friend won't suggest anything, say, "Okay, then, I'm going to the market to get some fresh vegetables, and I'm going to make you a big pot of homemade soup." Who can resist that? It's likely she'll join you in the kitchen, and the two of you can chop and talk to your hearts' content, and her family will have a nice soup for dinner.

8. Take your old magazines to someone who could use them (a shut-in, someone in the hospital, someone who loves to read but can't afford magazines, or a teenager who might like to clip photos or phrases for a scrapbook). A subscription to a magazine you know your friend will enjoy makes a welcome birthday or Christmas gift.

9. Forgive. Decide today that you will forgive that person who has offended you, even if he has never apologized. Forgive and forget it. Replace those feelings of anger, resentment, or revenge with the sweet, peaceful feeling that accompanies ridding your heart of such negative thoughts. Get over it and then do something nice for your former enemy. Your apology and gesture of

reconciliation may not be reciprocated, but the act of forgiving will lift the burden from you.

Harboring ill will is bad for your health. It takes a lot of time and energy to ignore and/or avoid people. Just because the other person behaved poorly doesn't mean you have to stoop to his level. Be the better person. How you do it is up to you. You can call, visit, meet for lunch—whatever is most comfortable for you. You don't even have to apologize (unless you caused the rift in the first place). You just need to say something like, "I've been feeling bad about what has happened to our relationship and would like to put our issues behind us. Do you think we can agree to disagree and not bring up that particular issue again? I'd still like to consider you a friend. Is that possible?" Try to talk it out without hashing over the old hurts. Rather than saying, "You did this and you did that," say things such as, "I felt hurt because . . . , and I miss . . ." It's easier if the other person never knew you were upset. In that case, you don't even have to bring the issue up. Just forget about it and go back to treating the person the way you did before. Make peace. You'll be glad you did.

10. Pay a compliment. Think about the qualities you admire in the people you know, and tell them. When someone looks good, say so. But don't go overboard on this. If you walk up to a group of friends and say to Judy, "I love your hair," and to Jane, "I love your dress," and to Andrea, "Cute shoes," you may come off

looking as though you are trying too hard. If they all look great, you can say, "You all look so good!" It is better to make compliments one on one. Above all, be genuine and sincere. People quickly see through and resent false expressions of admiration. When someone compliments you, learn to say, "Thank you." Don't tarnish the compliment by saying, "This old thing?" or "You need to have your eyes examined," or some other self-deprecating remark.

Be generous in your praise. When someone helps

you with a project, compliment him for a job well done. If a friend gets a promotion or recognition of some kind, send a congratulatory note praising her accomplishment.

If you happen to run across a photo or a mention of one of your friend's children in the local newspaper, clip it out and send it to her. If one of them enjoys some success in school or athletics or church, send a note or make a phone call congratulating the parent. People love it when you praise their kids.

Keep your jealousy in check. It's hard to congratulate a friend who has just won the lottery, but a true friend gives support both in times of sorrow and in times of joy and celebration.

11. If you are a religious person, pray for those about whom you are concerned. By just doing this simple task you will feel more love for them. Later, when you are able to do more, you will do it with even greater love in your heart. This is a wonderful thing that can be done by people who are not able to get out to serve others.

12. Invite your friend, or someone you'd like to be friends with, to join you when you jog, walk, ride bikes (your own or rent), play tennis, play golf, or try something new such as roller skating.

Go ice skating.

Go on a picnic in the park or at the lake or beach.

Visit an art museum.

Go to a benefit luncheon, home tour, etc.

Go to church or church activities.

Attend a fair or festival—there are interesting festivals all over the country: strawberry, garlic, carrot, frog jumping, etc. (Check *Sunset Magazine*).

Go to a rodeo.

Go to the hairdresser and get your friend an appointment at the same time. Maybe have lunch afterwards.

Go shopping.

Go to the movies, attend a concert, go for a drive, or attend a ball game.

13. Tend children so your friend can get away for awhile. This is something that is always appreciated and yet is so hard to have to ask for. If you know your friend is under pressure and needs to get away for a few hours, call and offer to be of service. You can go to her house or have her drop her kids off at your house. You could offer to take her kids to a movie or to the park for a picnic. December is an especially good month to offer to tend children so that the parents can shop for Christmas gifts. If you also have children, this provides your children with playmates and an unexpected adventure.

14. Offer to pick up a carpool or drive children to their after-school activities. This works like the above to provide reciprocal relief. If your friend will be away and the children are with a baby sitter who is unfamiliar with the children's routine, you could offer to do these chores, and the baby sitter, as well as your friend, will be grateful.

15. Offer to drive your friend to the hospital, doctor appointments, etc. A woman may occasionally have a surgical procedure that would make it difficult if not impossible for her to drive home from the hospital or clinic. Rather than have her husband take time off work, you could offer to drive her. A woman who is undergoing cancer treatments is usually able to drive, but would probably rather not. Perhaps she would appreciate having a good friend along as moral support. Be that friend.

16. Offer to do the grocery shopping. Say, “Hi, I’m on my way to the grocery store. Make a list and I’ll do yours while I'm there." This works better than, "Can I get you anything?" Make your offer easy to accept, and your friend will be less likely to turn you down. Keep the groceries separate so you can give her the actual sales slip and not have to guess at what she owes you. If you are just picking up some milk and bread, say, "It's on me."

17. Deliver a basket of fruits or vegetables from your garden along with a recipe for how to prepare the item. For example, a bunch of rhubarb and a recipe card for rhubarb pie or jam might be welcomed. Be sure to bring your gift in something that doesn't have to be returned to you. Even a brown paper sack can be attractive if it is tied with some ribbon. Some figs on a paper plate would look even more appealing if surrounded by a few nasturtiums or pansies.

18. Take a jar of whatever you are canning: salsa, hot pepper jelly, peaches, jam, pickles, etc. It's an easy thing to do, and it is so nice to receive a homemade jelly and not have to put up with the fuss of making it. This kind of gift is so much more than just a jar of jelly. It is a gift of your time and thoughtfulness. For Christmas, why not have a canning exchange, like people do cookie exchanges? You could each make up your favorite item and share your bounty.

19. Pass on a favorite book. When I read a book I really like, I have to tell everyone about it. But I have friends who can't afford to buy books. They have to wait until it hits the local library. Why wait? If you have such a friend, pass your favorites along. You could also work out a deal with a friend where you sit down together and decide what you want to read, then you buy half and he buys half. That way you can afford to read twice as many books as you could if you had to pay for each

one. Book fairs are another way to save on books you never got a chance to read. Invite your friend to go exploring with you and make a fun day of it.

20. Offer to water plants, pick up the newspaper, and/or feed pets when your neighbors go on vacation. This is another one of those situations where people really need the service, but they don't want to have to ask someone to do it for them. If you know your

neighbors will be away, offer to look after their property while they are gone. If you happen to have teenagers, give them the opportunity to serve. Just be sure to keep a watchful eye to make sure they perform the task.

21.

Keep track of birthdays of friends and send a card or telephone them. I like to call and sing "Happy Birthday." My sisters and I have been doing this for over thirty years. I always look forward to the phone call, and

it's more dependable than the mail. Have cards on hand (and stamps) to send for any occasion, so when you want to send a card, you can. I keep about 25 cards filed in a shoe box with index cards separating them into categories: birthdays, sympathy, thank-you, get well, hospital, baby, wedding, miscellaneous. Keep a supply of blank cards in which you can write your own message. There is something lovely and gracious about a handwritten note, personalized to fit the situation. You might also send a funny card for no reason, just to let your friend know you are thinking of her. Remember, cards are "hugs" in the mail.

22. Everyone has a birthday, and the way it is observed can be quite predictable. If you really want to do something extraordinary for your friend, give her a card on her birthday with a note in it telling her that this year she will get to celebrate all year long. Then, each month, on the day of her birthday, send a funny

card, visit, take her out to lunch, or bring a yummy treat (homemade is even better). I had a friend do this for me once, and I really looked forward to the 9th of every month.

23. An earthenware plate with printing that says "You are Special" can be purchased in many stores. It makes a great gift, and your friend can use it in her family to reward her children's accomplishments by letting them eat off the special plate on their birthdays, when they get good grades, or on any occasion where she would like to make a child feel special.

24. Pick up the phone and call a friend to say you are thinking about her. Perhaps you have a friend you haven't heard from in a long time. It's so nice to reestablish those old connections. Aren't there lots of people you think of from time to time and wonder how

they are doing? People you used to work with, neighbors who have moved away, parents of your children's friends who you were once close to. Stop wondering and find out. Chances are, they've been wondering about you, too. There is nothing quite like the glow that accompanies rekindling an old friendship.

25. "Doorbell Ditch." Leave a paper plate with any homemade goodie on someone's doorstep. Ring the bell and run like crazy so the family doesn't know who left it. Can you imagine them trying to guess who might be their benefactor? As they are driving or walking through the neighborhood or sitting in church on Sunday, they'll be wondering who cared enough to deliver the gift. Kids love to speculate in this way.

26. Pack a basket full of delicious herbal tea, teacups, teapot, tea sandwiches and sweets, a tablecloth, napkins, and flowers and have a "tea party." You can do it in your friend's kitchen, dining room, backyard, or in a park. Include a gift box of the tea you selected or a cup and saucer as a remembrance of the day.

27. Ask your friend to let you know when his car needs servicing, and help out by driving it to and from the service department. Getting a car serviced is always such a nuisance. We tend to put it off as long as possible because we don't want to impose on our friends for a ride. Let your friend know that you are waiting for that call.

28. If you have artistic talent, create something special for your friend. For example, knit or crochet an Afghan, tie a quilt, hand paint a box, cover a box with buttons, jewels, etc., make a watercolor or oil painting, put together a floral arrangement, create a holiday decoration or a Christmas tree ornament, decorate an Easter egg, write a poem, or frame a picture or a photograph.

29. Does your friend collect anything? Add to her collection (or start one) with frogs, butterfly pins, cats, bees, swans, pigs, elephants, cows, teacups, teapots, commemorative plates, spoons, rocks, shells, stamps, coins, recipe books, matchbooks, pipes, putters, or tools. The list is endless. Half the fun I have while traveling is shopping in gift stores to bring back a little something for my friends. I feel myself a part of their collection by adding to it. I'm always on the lookout for something cute for my buddies.

30. Bake a pie and go to an antique shop and buy a crocheted round to put it on. You should be able to find one for under $10. I got this idea from a friend. She always leaves her back door open, and one day she came home and found a homemade apple pie on her kitchen table. It was sitting on a beautiful crocheted round. She was ecstatic, and I was impressed with the giver's creativity. It is truly amazing what we can come up with if we give something a little thought.

31. Take your friend a dessert (purchase a special pan to bake it in and give it as part of the gift) or cookies (on a platter with her name engraved on it). I've seen really cute muffin tins and heart-shaped cake pans that would make great gifts. Trendy hardware and kitchen

stores have a variety of darling covered casserole containers that would be cute to give as a thank-you to a hostess or for a housewarming gift or a birthday remembrance. You could bake a favorite casserole in the dish and deliver it. Be sure to let your friend know if the serving piece is a gift for her. (Hint: When you take food to friends, either put it in a container that doesn't need to be returned to you or be sure to come back within the week to pick up the container. Don't make it your friend's responsibility to get it back to you. If you want

the serving dish back, it is a good idea to put your name on it. I usually put a piece of scotch tape on the bottom of the dish and write my name on it—in indelible ink, so if it gets wet the name doesn't wash off.)

32. Take dinner to your friend. Contact a few friends and each of you bring part of the dinner. This is a great thing to do for someone who has just had a baby, surgery, or a death in the family. There are times

when cooking is just not possible, and there are only so many nights the family can put up with pizza delivery. There's nothing better than having a good home-cooked meal show up. Call and ask what time the family likes to have dinner. That way they know it's coming and when to expect it (so they don't call the pizza man or fill up on junk food).

33. Invite your friend to breakfast, lunch, or dinner. It can be in your home, at a park, or at some quaint out-of-the-way restaurant you have discovered. Make it a party and invite a few friends. If you don't want an argument over the check, make certain your guest knows the treat is on you.

34. Plan a "get away" for just the two of you or add a friend. A day in the city. Two or three days at a local resort. A three-day cruise. An overnighter at a beach house. A sleep-over at a mountain cabin. A ski trip. Attend a seminar. You really get to know a person when you spend a couple of days with her. It's a chance to get beyond the small talk and find out who she is from the inside out. It provides the best bonding opportunity ever.

35. Invite your friend to take a class with you. Aerobics, painting, crafts, CPR, cooking—anything you both find interesting. Check at a community college or YWCA for a catalog of classes offered. You can kill two birds with one stone: you improve your own skills and you form a bond with another person. This might be especially welcomed by a person who is not self-motivated. If your friend knows you are depending on her to be there, she'll likely make the effort to attend the class instead of rationalizing why today is not a good day.

36. Start a "Gourmet Dinner Group" with three other couples (include spouses). Start by getting together for dinner four times a year, each couple taking turns acting as hosts once during the year. The hosts provide the house, the main entree (meat & vegetable), and the beverage. The other members each bring a part of the meal: rolls, appetizer, salad, and dessert. Go all out. You might like this so much you'll make it a monthly event. Men love a great meal and most don't mind small groups. It's a nice opportunity for the men to talk sports or business while the ladies are in the kitchen (or vice versa!).

37. Go out of your way to be the first to welcome a newcomer into the neighborhood, the workplace, church, school, or a club or spa. It isn't necessary to take a goodie, but such a gesture is always appreciated. At the very least, inquire about her interests, offer to be of assistance, ask about family and background, and introduce her to others. Anticipate questions and offer help: where do you grocery shop, where are the nearby schools or churches or post office, what about public transportation? Above all, be friendly. Going into a new situation is often very traumatic. To find even one friendly, helpful person can make a huge difference. Be that person.

38. How long has it been since you've done something unexpected for your children? If they are still in the lunch box stage, enclose a little note telling them how special they are. My daughters used to carry their lunch in paper sacks. To mark the bags, I would draw a picture of each one with whatever hairstyle they had and what clothes they were wearing that day (just circle face, head, and shoulders, nothing fancy). It made it easy for them to identify their lunch and if they left it some-

where, their friends or their teacher could easily get it back to them. If they are teenagers, leave sticky notes on their mirror or in their car telling them how proud you are of the choices they are making. If your children are away at college, send them a box of their favorite treats.

39. Send a little gift in the mail. Who doesn't like to get a package in the mail? "Oooh, I wonder who this is from?" "I wonder what it is?" It's like getting an extra day of Christmas. It tells a person that someone is thinking about her and that she is special—special enough for you to go to the trouble of selecting something for her and mailing it to her. Shopping is even easier now with the Internet. You can shop online for almost anything. They'll even gift-wrap and send it for you with a card. It doesn't have to be for a special occasion. If you see something you know your friend would like, maybe a book you've talked about or a cookbook from her favorite restaurant, send it with a note: "I just couldn't resist. I knew you'd love this. Thanks for being my friend."

40. Send flowers, or bring them in person. They don't have to be from a florist—they can be hand-picked from your garden. Too ordinary, you say? Not necessarily. Did you know there is a whole language of flowers? When florists advertise, "Say it with flowers," they mean it *literally*. Do a search on the Internet for "meaning of

flowers." There are many sites that explain what certain flowers and colors mean. A variety of flowers can be combined in a bouquet to express your sentiments exactly. For example, lilies of the valley represent unconscious sweetness, and ferns mean fascination. Your card might read, "Your unconscious sweetness fascinates me."

Different sites on the web attribute different meanings to the flowers and their colors, so be sure the card you send includes an explanation of what each flower represents. For instance; a red rose can symbolize bashful shame, beauty, or love. A yellow rose can mean love or friendship. Here are some of my favorite meanings:

ROSES represent love

- Red (beauty)
- Pink (happiness)
- Yellow (friendship)
- White (I am worthy of you, or purity)
- White and red roses together (unity)

CARNATIONS represent fascination (Note: on Mother's or Father's day, a red carnation is worn to signify that the parent is living, a white carnation indicates that the parent is deceased).

- Pink (friendship)

CHRYSANTHEMUMS suggest "You are a wonderful friend."

- Red (I love you)
- White (truth)

DAISIES represent innocence.

LILIES stand for remembrance.

- White (sweetness)
- Yellow ("Have a happy day.")

PANSIES say, "I am thinking of you."

SWEET PEAS say, "I'll miss you. Thanks for the wonderful time."

LILACS suggest, "I think I love you."

IRISES say, "I have a message for you."
- Yellow (passion)

IVY stands for fidelity, marriage.

DAFFODILS signal, "Best wishes. The sun always shines when I am with you."

ORCHIDS represent beauty, thoughtfulness.

TULIPS represent love and say, "Good luck!"

When someone does something especially nice for you, in addition to flowers you might want to send a note or a box of candy. If your friend won't, or can't, eat candy, send a candy box full of golf balls, CDs, jewelry, etc. Gift certificates for a dinner for two, a box of nice stationery, a spa treatment, and movie passes are also fun to receive.

41. If a family you know is low on cash, you don't want to insult them by giving money, but there are still ways you can help. Hire them to perform a service: "I'll give you fifty dollars if you'll drive my carpool this month," or hire one of their teenagers to perform a service: "I'd be willing to pay Johnny forty dollars a week to mow my lawn." If you really want to give money, do it anonymously. If they know it is from you, they likely won't take it. Send a Christmas card "from Santa" saying: "Santa knows you could use a little cash this year. Merry Christmas!" If they would recognize your handwriting, type the message. It defeats the whole purpose if they can figure it out.

42. Clever, inexpensive gifts:

• Give a box of "cheer." Use an empty Cheer detergent box. Put things in it that will make your friend smile, such as a photo of the two of you doing something silly, a favorite candy or cookies, a joke book, or a gag gift.

• Bake a cake and attach a note saying "You take the cake." Or make it an angel food cake and write "You're an angel."

• Prepare a basket of really fattening goodies with a note saying "I've gained so much from our friendship . . . now it's your turn."

• Give a jar of freshly cracked nuts with a note saying "I'd go nuts without you."

• Make some jam and attach a note saying "Thanks for getting me out of a jam!"

A pot of homemade soup might have a note attached: "You're a souper friend!."

43. If you are a close enough friend, ask her for her car keys, then get her car washed and gassed. This is a nice gesture anytime, but it is especially nice if there is a big occasion coming up, such as a prom, a night on the town, a benefit, a wedding, or a funeral—any event where she would like to have the car looking good but

won't have time to wash it. Just imagine how grateful you'd be if someone did this for you.

44. Donate your old clothes to the Salvation Army, Goodwill Industries, St. Vincent de Paul's, Deseret Industries, or your local thrift shop. If you haven't worn something for the last two years, what makes you think you'll wear it next year? You will

probably never know who's wearing your donation, but rest assured someone will be happier for it.

45. Join a volunteer organization. If you don't know what you would like to do, start reading the social columns of your local newspaper. They are filled with news regarding your local charity organizations. Find one that appeals to you. Look at the photos. Are you about the same age as the members? Would you enjoy working on their fund raiser? If so, contact any of the names listed in the article. They would love to have you. Don't be discouraged if they put you off a few months. Some groups only take in new members during a certain month of the year. It's not you—it's their bylaws.

46. Donate blood. Call your local Blood Bank, community hospital, or the American Red Cross. There is an ongoing, never-ending need for blood. Supplies often dwindle and are dangerously low from time to time. If you know you have a surgery coming up where you might need blood, you can donate your own blood. If you have a friend who is in the hospital and may need a transfusion, offer to donate blood. Blood cannot be manufactured. It can only come from a donor. Giving blood really is a way to give the gift of life.

47. If your friend has been diagnosed with a disease, educate yourself on that disease. There are hundreds of excellent books to choose from. Check the bookstores in your area. If you can't afford to buy a book, check your local library, or look up the disease on the Internet. The more you know, the more help you will be to your friend. He has a right to a second opinion. Encourage him to seek one from someone who specializes in that particular disease. Once he has selected the doctor and the treatment, respect his decision. Don't say, "I think you should check out Dr. . . . ," or, "So and so is doing such and such a treatment; you should try it." There are almost always treatment options. If your friend has heard all the options before deciding on his treatment, don't impose your own opinions to the contrary.

48. Become an organ donor. In the event that something should happen to you, you can help someone else. There are thousands of people on waiting lists for organs that would save their lives. The family members you leave behind will feel better knowing that a part of you is still living and that someone else who would have died is alive because of your donation. Imagine what the gift of sight, a kidney, liver, or even skin might mean to someone whose life or happiness hangs in the balance. It is easy to do. Most states have a box that you can check when you apply for your driver's license. You can even specify which organs you are willing to donate. Or, simply write your wishes on a piece of paper and have it signed by two witnesses. Let your family know of your decision and where you keep the signed document in case it is required in your state.

49. Reach out and touch someone. Most people love to be touched. There is something wonderfully comforting about holding hands, receiving a warm hug, walking arm in arm, or even getting a gentle pat on the back or shoulder. It is connecting. I'm not talking about making a pest of yourself. You don't want people to run the other way when they see you coming. In these days of hightened political correctness and sensitivity to sexual harassment, be careful. Be aware that some people are jealous of their space and don't want anyone intruding into it. If someone backs up as you approach her, that is your clue to back off. (A gentle reminder here: if you are the huggy-kissy type, be sure your breath is fresh. There's nothing worse than someone who gets in your face with garlic breath.)

50. Think of strangers as family you haven't met yet. Be excited to meet new people. Being genuinely interested in other people makes them feel special, and they will feel closer to you. If it is difficult for you to extend yourself due to shyness, think how you would appreciate someone befriending you if you were the stranger. A smile, a warm handshake, and a friendly greeting cost you nothing and may make all the difference to someone struggling to fit into a new situation.

51. Stop thinking in terms of doing things that are important to you and start doing things because you know they are important to someone else. It is easy to get locked into our own little sphere, to focus solely on our own needs and responsibilities. For many of us it requires a conscious effort to extend ourselves, to find time to help, express concern, or perform a service. Yet these are the things we can do to help lift someone else and, curiously enough, secure our own happiness and sense of worth.

52. Practice the Golden Rule. No, not the one that says "He who has the gold makes the rules," but the *original* one: "Do unto others as you would have them do unto you." Treat others the way you would want them to treat you. That's the great secret to happiness.